Pronto Pizazz

VOLUME ONE

Easy Solos with Energy & Style

Music by

Jennifer Eklund

PIANO PRONTO PUBLISHING

PianoPronto.com

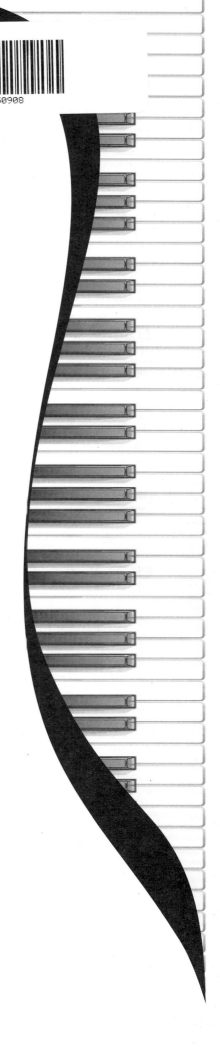

Pronto Pizazz: Volume One

Jennifer Eklund

Copyright © 2014 by Jennifer Eklund. All Rights Reserved.

WARNING: The compositions, arrangements, text, and graphics in this publication are protected by copyright law. No part of this work may be duplicated or reprinted without the prior consent of the author.

ISBN 978-0-9899084-9-8

Printed in the United States of America

Piano Pronto Publishing
PianoPronto.com

Cover Design: Chaz DeSimone
Author Photo: Nancy Villere

Pronto Pizazz

VOLUME ONE

Easy Solos with Energy & Style

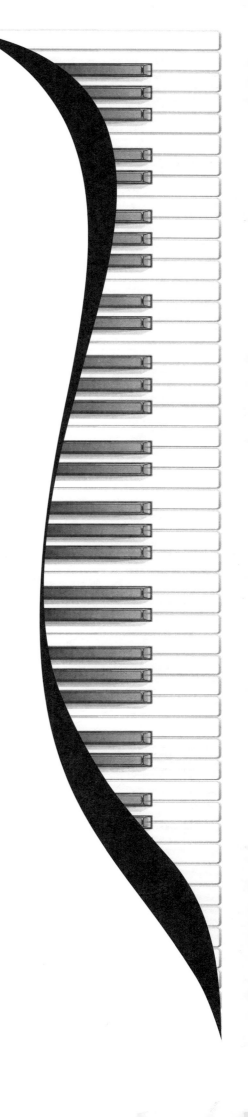

Off to the Races 4
Shall We Dance? 6
Cheers! 8
Rising Star 10
Creepy Crawlers 12
Hop, Skip, and a Jump 14
Down a Country Road 16
Catch Me If You Can 18
Little Serenade 22
Roll the Dice 24
Strolling 26
Jazz Cat 32
Out of the Fog 34
Rockin' the Boat 36
Someday 38
A Minor Mystery 42

Music by
Jennifer Eklund

PIANO PRONTO PUBLISHING

PianoPronto.com

Off to the Races
Student Part

Quickly
Play 1 octave higher

Jennifer Eklund

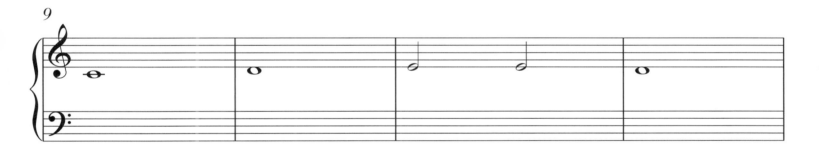
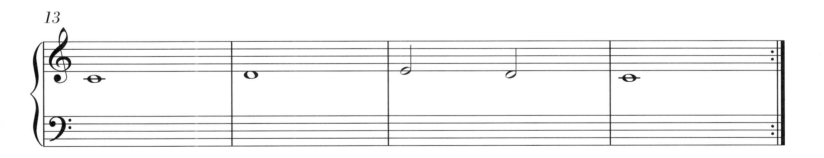
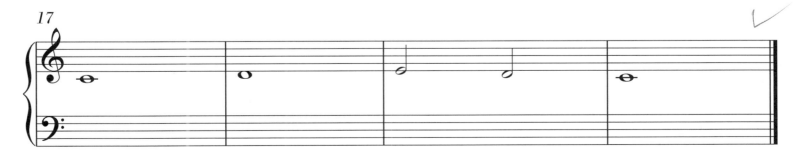

Shall We Dance?
Student Part

Gracefully
Play 1 octave higher

Jennifer Eklund

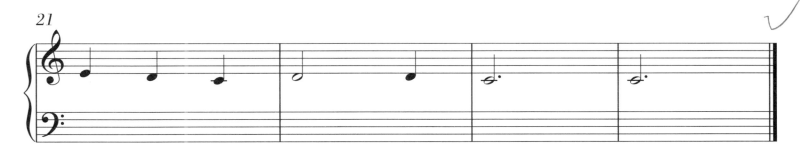

Copyright © 2014 Piano Pronto Publishing
All Rights Reserved | PianoPronto.com

Cheers!
Student Part

Joyfully
Play 2 octaves higher

Swedish Traditional
Arr. Jennifer Eklund

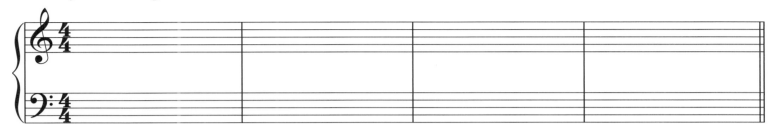

Copyright © 2014 Piano Pronto Publishing
All Rights Reserved | PianoPronto.com

Rising Star
Teacher Part

Rising Star
Student Part

Jennifer Eklund

Copyright © 2014 Piano Pronto Publishing
All Rights Reserved | PianoPronto.com

Creepy Crawlers

Teacher Part

Creepy Crawlers
Student Part

Jennifer Eklund

Hop, Skip, and a Jump
Student Part

Jennifer Eklund

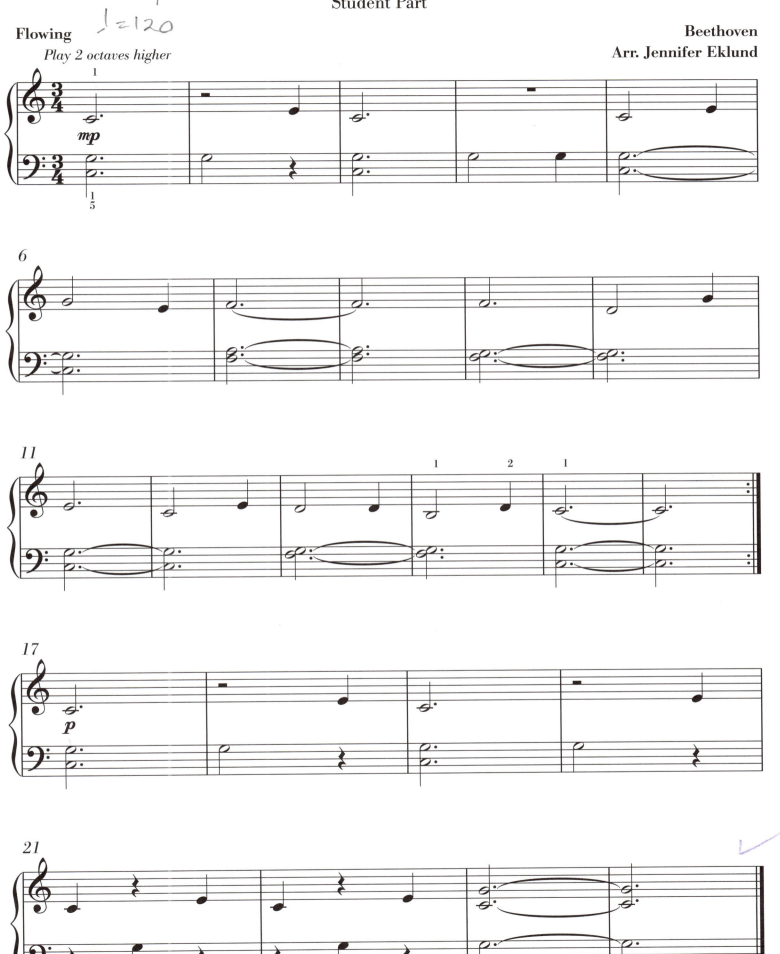

Catch Me If You Can
Teacher Part

Quickly
Play as written

Jennifer Eklund

Catch Me If You Can
Student Part

Quickly
Play 2 octaves higher

Jennifer Eklund

Student Part

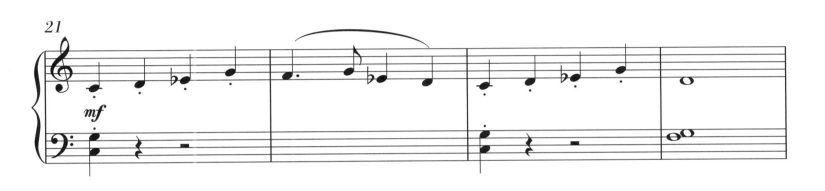
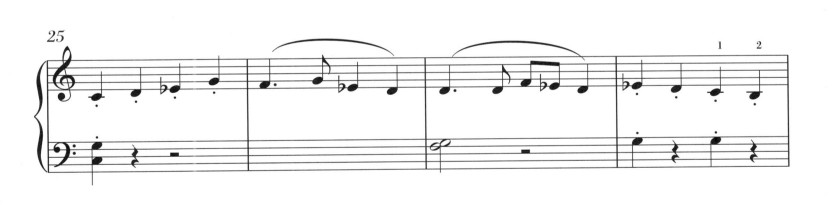

Little Serenade
Teacher Part

Moderately
Play as written

Jennifer Eklund

Little Serenade
Student Part

Jennifer Eklund

Strolling
Teacher Part

Moderately fast
Play as written

Jennifer Eklund

Strolling
Student Part

Moderately fast
Play 1 or 2 octaves higher

Jennifer Eklund

1/10/20

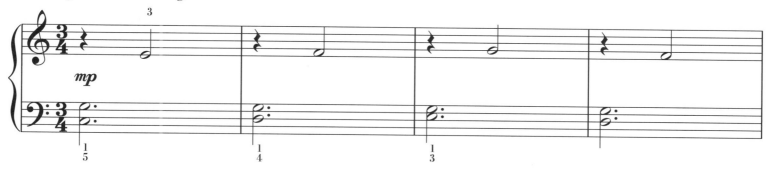

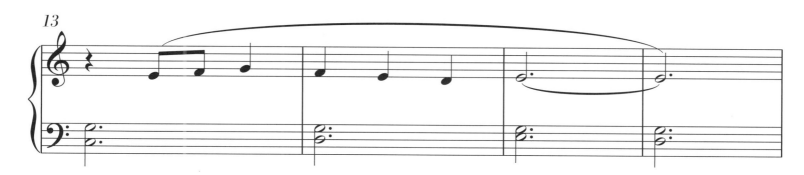

Student Part

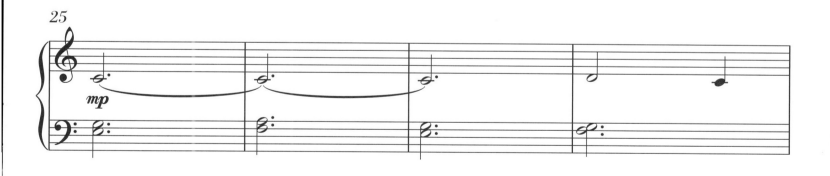
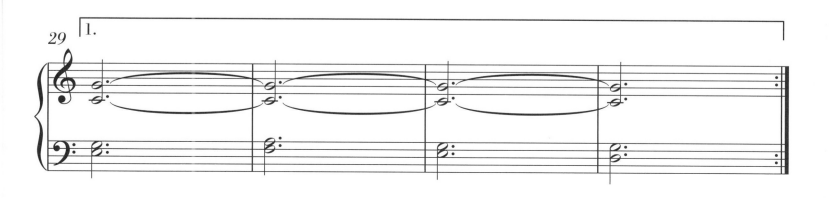

Teacher Part

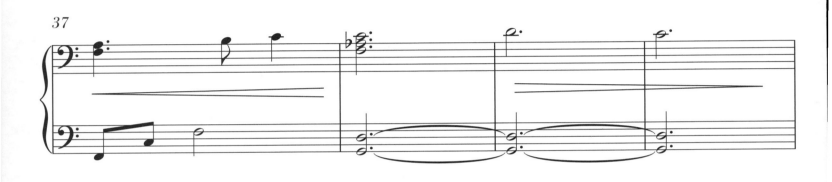

Student Part

Jazz Cat
Teacher Part

Jennifer Eklund

Moderate swing
Play as written

Jazz Cat
Student Part

Moderate swing
Play 2 octaves higher

Jennifer Eklund

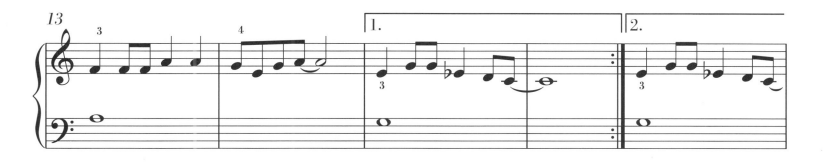

Out of the Fog
Student Part

Jennifer Eklund

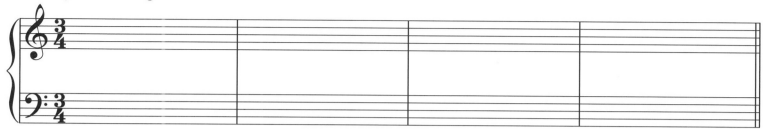
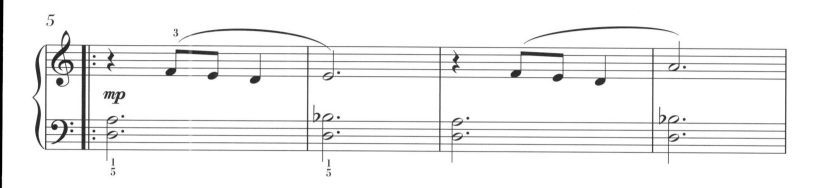
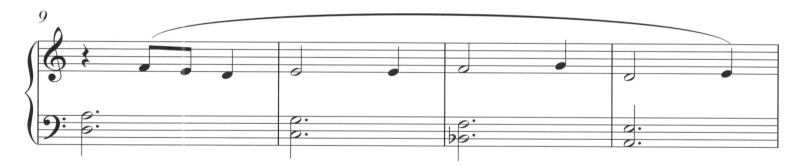
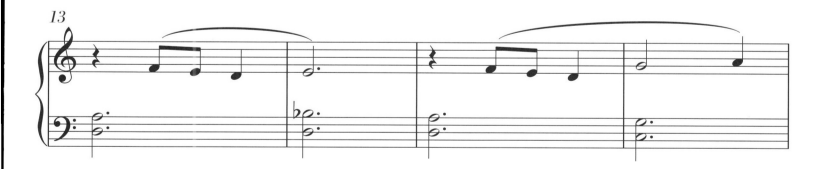

Rockin' the Boat
Teacher Part

Jennifer Eklund

Someday
Teacher Part

Jennifer Eklund

Moderately
Play as written

Someday
Student Part

Jennifer Eklund

Moderately
Play 2 octaves higher

15/10/20
♩=110

Teacher Part

A Minor Mystery
Teacher Part

Jennifer Eklund

Moderately fast
Play as written

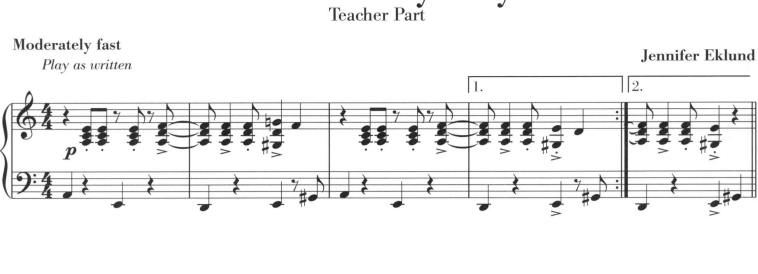

A Minor Mystery
Student Part

Moderately fast
Play 2 octaves higher

Jennifer Eklund

Teacher Part

Student Part

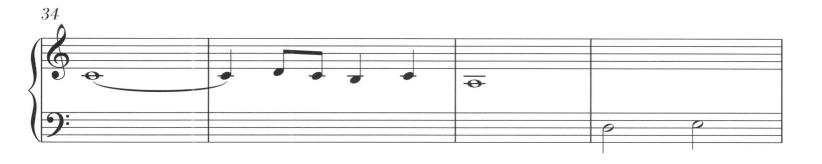

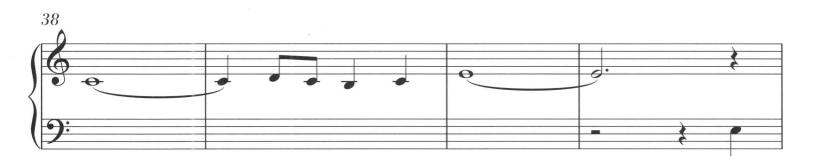

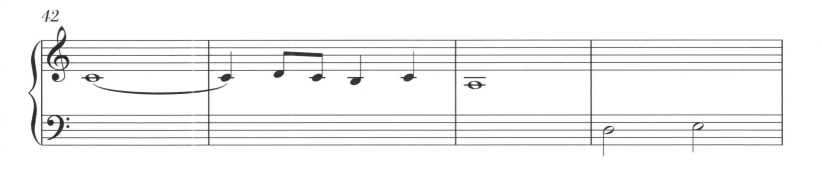

Teacher Part

Student ad lib. using A minor pentascale

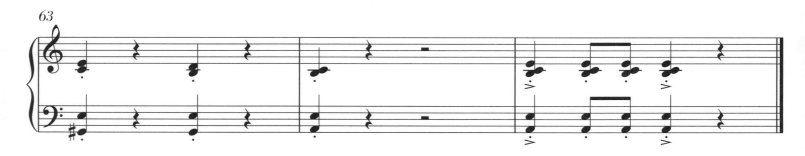

*Suggested length 32 measures or teacher can play the accompaniment part only

Student Part

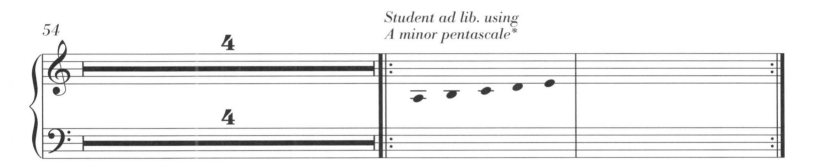

*Student ad lib. using
A minor pentascale**

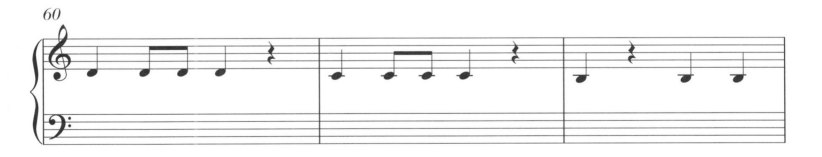

Suggested length 32 measures

PIANO PRONTO